THE LOVED ONES

by Erica Murray

FOR AMATEUR PRODUCTION ENQUIRIES

UNITED KINGDOM AND WORLD
EXCLUDING NORTH AMERICA
licensing@concordtheatricals.co.uk
020-7054-7298

Each title is subject to availability from Concord Theatricals, depending upon country of performance.

USE OF COPYRIGHTED MUSIC

USE OF COPYRIGHTED THIRD-PARTY MATERIALS

IMPORTANT BILLING AND CREDIT REQUIREMENTS

The Loved Ones was commissioned by Rough Magic as part of its COMPASS programme, and received its world premiere in a co-production between Rough Magic and the Gate Theatre at the Gate Theatre, Dublin on 2 October 2023. The cast, creative team and production team were as follows:

NELL . . . . Jane Brennan
GABBY . . . . Fanta Barrie
CHERYL-ANN . . . . Helen Norton
ORLA . . . . Gráinne Keenan

Director . . . . Ronan Phelan
Designer . . . . Sarah Bacon
Lighting Designer . . . . Zia Bergin-Holly
Composer and Sound Designer . . . . Tom Lane
Assistant Director (SEEDS) . . . . Joy Nesbitt
Assistant Costume Designer (SEEDS) . . . . Toni Bailey
Assistant Sound Designer (SEEDS) . . . . HK Ní Shioradáin
Assistant Set Designer (THE LIR) . . . . Chrysi Chatzivasileiou

Production Manager . . . . Eamonn Fox
Stage Manager . . . . Donna Leonard
Assistant Stage Manager . . . . Sarah Purcell
Costume Supervisor . . . . Aoife Eustace-Doyle
Hair and Make Up . . . . Sarah McCann
Dresser . . . . Sarah Higgins

For Rough Magic
Artistic Director . . . . Lynne Parker
General Manager . . . . Gemma Reeves
Producer . . . . Sara Cregan

For The Gate Theatre
Artistic Director . . . . Róisín McBrinn
Executive Director . . . . Colm O'Callaghan
Head of Producing . . . . Kate Ferris
Associate Producer . . . . Michelle King
Producing and Programming Assistant . . . . Chloe Ní Mhurchú
Head of Audience & Media . . . . Stephen Boylan
Audience & Media Marketing Manager . . . . Dara O'Donnell
Publicist . . . . Kate Bowe
Interim Head of Production and Operations . . . . Marty Moore
Head of Costume . . . . James McGlynn Seaver

ROUGH

MAGIC

Rough Magic is a national, independent theatre company, delivering a comprehensive programme of new Irish writing, reimagined classics, and contemporary international plays, to audiences across Ireland and beyond. Our work is expansive, playful and whatever its form, focused on the moment. Rough Magic provides an unexpected angle to the mainstream and an anchor to the emerging generation.

Over four decades, Rough Magic has established itself as a creative entity and a valued institution; operating as an ensemble across the spectrum of scale and style, offering fresh perspectives and engaging audiences with the qualities that define us – wit, subversion, intellectual rigour, and free artistic expression. Since its foundation in 1984, Rough Magic has produced 139 shows, including 43 World premieres and 26 Irish premieres.

The company is an industry pioneer in artist development, notably through our SEEDS programme for emerging artists, through which many leading theatre makers were introduced to the industry. We believe in showcasing and platforming theatre practitioners at all stages, supporting them to take artistic risks.

In 2021 the company launched COMPASS, folding play development and support for theatre artists into the company's core programme. Under COMPASS we have established partnerships with leading theatres in Limerick, Waterford and Cork to produce a series of major new commissions as we approach our 40th Anniversary. *The Loved Ones* by Erica Murray is the first of these commissions to come to the stage, in a co-production with the Gate Theatre, Dublin, supported by our partners at Lime Tree | Belltable, Limerick.

Awards include: a record number of four Irish Times Theatre Awards for Best Production (*Copenhagen, Improbable Frequency, The Taming of the Shrew, Don Carlos*); London Time Out Award; two Edinburgh Fringe First Awards and the Irish Times Theatre Award for Best Ensemble for *A Midsummer Night's Dream*. Most recently Rough Magic's production of *Solar Bones* won Best Actor for Stanley Townsend and Best Director for Lynne Parker at the Irish Times Theatre Awards.

Rough Magic is proudly supported by the Arts Council.

THEATRE

The Gate Theatre was founded in 1928 in Dublin by Hilton Edwards and Micheál Mac Liammóir. Pioneers in both their professional and personal lives, their productions were innovative and experimental, offering audiences an introduction to European and American theatre as well as classics from the Irish repertoire.

During their first season they presented ambitious productions of Ibsen's *Peer Gynt*, Eugene O'Neill's *The Hairy Ape* and Wilde's *Salomé*. On 17th February 1930, the Gate moved to its present location on Cavendish Row with a production of Goethe's *Faust*.

To this day, the Gate Theatre remains an artist-led organisation producing world class original work which inspires, challenges and entertains our audiences.

The Gate develops and supports emerging and established practitioners with the ambition and talent to produce new work, alongside reinvigorating existing work from the Irish and international canon.

Led by Artistic Director Róisín McBrinn and Executive Director Colm O'Callaghan, the ethos and vision of the Gate demands that it fulfils its social and cultural purpose as an international home for Irish artists and an Irish home for international artists, creating a 'world theatre' limited only, as Edwards said, by the limits of its imagination.

For more news on how to support the Gate's work, and for information on upcoming productions, visit www.gatetheatre.ie.

The Gate Theatre is proudly supported by the Arts Council.

EXECUTIVE

Artistic Director / Co-CEO	Róisín McBrinn
Executive Director / Co-CEO	Colm O'Callaghan
Executive Assistant	Jack Savage

PRODUCING AND ARTISTIC

Head of Producing	Kate Ferris
Associate Producer	Michelle King
Producing and Programming Assistant	Chloe Ní Mhurchú

| Resident Assistant Director | Ciara Fleming |
| Company Stage Manager | Cian Mulhall |

MARKETING AND COMMUNICATIONS

Head of Audience & Media	Stephen Boylan
Audience & Media Marketing Manager	Dara O'Donnell
Audience & Media Marketing Assistant	Niamh Martin
Publicist	Kate Bowe

DEVELOPMENT AND COMMUNITY ENGAGEMENT

| Head of Development | Eimear Chaomhánach |
| Community Engagement Manager | John Taite |

HR AND FINANCE

Head of HR	Catherine Bannon
Head of Finance	Orlagh Murphy
Finance Assistant	Lisa Harrington
Payroll Officer	Gary Reilly
Accounts Assistant	Daniela Ramos

PRODUCTION

Interim Head of Production and Operations	Marty Moore
Production and Operations Co-Ordinator	Katie McGrath
Head of Costume	James McGlynn Seaver
Costume Supervisor	Aoife Eustace Doyle
Sound Technician	Andy Walsh
Lighting Technician	Rory Donnelly

OPERATIONS

Operations Manager	Anna Haslam
Front of House Manager	Vincent Brightling
Deputy Front of House Manager	John Murphy
Bar Manager	Cathal Maguire
Box Office Manager	Dave Fleming
Box Office Assistant	Faela Stafford
Café Supervisor	Síofra Brogan
Housekeeping	Cathy Mortimore
Maintenance	Tom Hogben

GUEST RELATIONS ASSISTANTS

Bianca Barchetta, Maeve Bradley, Cathal Brogan, Ava Byrne, Ana Canals
Ní Éigeartaigh, Luke Dalton, Muireann Guilfoyle, Ellie Henry, Hazel
Hogan, Darragh Feehely, Isabelle Hackett, Sarah Joan Kelly, Ella-Bleu
Kiely, Jacob McConnell, Conor McGowan, Matt McGowan, Daragh
McMahon, Shauna McNevin, Jacob Maguire, Lucas Maguire, Orla
Mooney, Lisa Nally, Micheál Ó Fearraigh, Daire O'Muirí, Síobhra Pringle,
Aoibhe Walsh, Molly Whelan, Sarah Wiley

ACKNOWLEDGEMENTS

I'd like to firstly say thank you to Rough Magic Theatre Company for commissioning and supporting *The Loved Ones* from its very first iteration. So, a huge thank you to Lynne Parker, Sara Cregan, Gemma Reeves, Karin McCully and Ronan Phelan for your enthusiasm and belief in the play. To Ronan, your love of the characters and unwavering conviction in the importance of this story has been fundamental.

Thank you to everyone at the Gate Theatre for such a warm welcome, especially Michelle King who made us feel right at home and looked after us from the start. A massive thank you to Róisín and Colm for seeing the potential in the script and deciding to platform it on the Gate stage. It is so exciting to be here.

A very special thank you to the incredible actors who brought the characters to life – Jane Brennan, Gráinne Keenan, Helen Norton and Fanta Barrie. I feel extremely lucky to be working with such talented, lovely people and have enjoyed watching you build the characters so much.

Thank you to our amazing design team; Sarah Bacon, Zia Bergin-Holly and Tom Lane for your incredibly detailed work and investment in the world of the play. Thank you to our brilliant stage managers Donna and Sarah who keep the show firmly on the road.

Thank you to all the wonderful actors who participated in early workshops of the draft; Clare Barrett, Gina Moxley, Aoibhéann McCann, Ciara Berkley, Olwen Fouéré, Lola Petticrew, Pollyanna McIntosh and Kathy-Rose O'Brien.

Thank you to all my lovely Six in the Attic crew and everyone at Irish Theatre Institute for being so supportive during this process; especially Niamh O'Donnell, Katherine Murphy, Leigh Hussey, Richie O'Sullivan and Gráinne Pollak.

Thank you to my fantastic agent and friend Jessi Stewart. And thank you to my two great playwright friends and cheerleaders Nancy Harris and David Ireland.

Thank you to my Mom for being my most enthusiastic and eagled-eyed reader through every draft.

Thank you to Finn, for being by my side.

CHARACTERS

NELL – 60s, Irish, Robin's mother. Old battered coat with a cashmere jumper underneath.

GABBY – early 20s, English. Seven months pregnant but not wearing maternity clothes.

CHERYL-ANN – 50s, American tourist, keen ornithologist. Wears a sweater that says "Expecto Patronum".

ORLA – late 30s, Irish, Robin's wife. Her clothes are always stylish and pristine.

SETTING

An open plan kitchen-living space in a renovated farmhouse in West Clare, Ireland.

TIME

Present day.

Important: Robin died six months ago.

PART ONE

(**NELL** *is standing in the middle of her kitchen. She has her work boots on and an old rain jacket, she was clearly not expecting visitors. She's staring at* **GABBY**, *who is standing awkwardly in the middle of the room, holding a backpack and a carry-on wheely suitcase.*)

(*The room is cluttered with items from years of different generations living here – ranging from fancy new Irish delph on the shelves to old woven blankets on the couch by the fire. It is an old house that has been renovated to suit modern living. It's tasteful, cosy, messy not dirty.*)

(*It is around eleven a.m. The weather is awful, a miserable rainy day in June.*)

GABBY. Seven months. I'm due at the end of August.

(*She waits for* **NELL** *to say something, but she doesn't.*)

Or maybe the middle of August. I couldn't remember the exact date of my last period and apparently, it's from then they count, not the date of actual conception, which still makes no sense to me.

(*Again, she looks at* **NELL** *to say something, again she doesn't.*)

1

We had a kind of on and off thing... I guess it was more on than off. We had tried to stop seeing each other. Then one evening, around Christmas I was walking through campus, and I saw he was in his office, alone. So, I called in to give him this book I knew he'd love and we...you know. That was the last time I saw him before he...

NELL. Died?

GABBY. Yeah.

> *(An awkward silence.)*

I'm really sorry for your loss by the way. Sorry, I probably should have said that first.

> (**NELL** *acknowledges this but doesn't say anything. Another silence.*)

So...this is where he grew up then?

NELL. Yes.

GABBY. Did he live here all his life?

NELL. Until he went to college. Yes.

GABBY. Wow.

NELL. What do you mean?

GABBY. Just so different from where I grew up.

NELL. And where was that?

GABBY. Lewisham.

NELL. I don't know it.

GABBY. Yeah, we were packed in like sardines. Still are. Can't imagine having all this space as a kid. Was it good?

NELL. Was what good?

GABBY. Like him having a basically endless garden?

NELL. Eh, I think so...we didn't really have any other option.

GABBY. Did he have any friends around or was it just the two of you for miles?

NELL. He had a friend down the road. They used to cycle their bikes together.

GABBY. Cool.

NELL. But, yes, a lot of the time it was just the two of us here.

GABBY. Wow. It's just so...isolated. You could run around naked and no one would see you.

NELL. We never did that.

GABBY. No, sorry.

(*A pause.*)

You should know that I really, really did not plan on this happening. It was a massive shock to me too when I found out.

NELL. And when was that?

GABBY. During my Easter holidays. April. I went to the doctor on campus cos I thought I had a stomach ulcer. Had one before, horrific. But yeah, she said I didn't have one of those but that I was five-months pregnant. So by then it was too late to do anything *drastic*, if you know what I mean?

NELL. I do.

GABBY. I'm aware this is literally a nightmare. Don't think I don't know that.

(**NELL** *pauses, weighing her up a bit.*)

NELL. Would you like a fresh egg?

GABBY. Sorry?

NELL. A fresh egg.

GABBY. Eh. What?

NELL. I've just collected them.

GABBY. Are you taking in anything I'm telling you here?

NELL. Oh, I am.

GABBY. Eh, right, alright then I'll have an egg?

> (**NELL** *fixes water in a saucepan for the eggs.*
> **GABBY** *takes off her backpack and leaves*
> *it neatly by her suitcase.* **NELL** *turns back*
> *around to face her, scrutinising her a bit*
> *more now.)*

NELL. So, you found out in April that you were pregnant?

GABBY. Yeah and by then Robin was...you know, not around.

NELL. And was there anyone else in the picture?

GABBY. *(Thrown.)* What do you mean?

NELL. Were you sleeping with anyone else at the time?

> *(A beat.)*

GABBY. Excuse me but I haven't travelled all this way to be slut shamed.

NELL. Slut, what?

GABBY. Slut shamed. You're slut shaming me.

NELL. I don't even know what that is?

GABBY. Just because I'm open about sleeping with your son doesn't mean I'm sleeping around or like I'd just have sex with anyone or whatever.

NELL. I didn't say that.

GABBY. You're judging me now. I can feel you judging me.

NELL. I'm really not.

GABBY. You're thinking, oh, look at this silly girl, knocked up by her uni lecturer, doesn't take herself seriously, doesn't give a shit about her education or want an actual career that'll take her places.

NELL. I am really not thinking any of that.

(Beat.)

GABBY. What are you thinking then?

NELL. I'm wondering how you're so sure it's Robin's baby.

(A pause. That's fair enough, I suppose.)

GABBY. Right, yeah, I guess because it was only him I was with. So basic maths; it could only be his. And before you ask, we were using protection every time. I'm not an idiot. And I was on the pill too, so we were *really* protected, if you know what I mean.

NELL. Look, Gabry –

GABBY. It's Gabby.

NELL. Gabby. I really don't think my son would do something like this.

GABBY. Like what?

NELL. Like sleep with his student.

GABBY. Really?

NELL. He wasn't that type of person.

GABBY. Eh...okay, I don't know what to tell you because, well, clearly, he was.

NELL. Maybe you're a bit confused?

GABBY. I'm not confused. I think you're a bit confused.

NELL. You see, Robin was very honest.

GABBY. I know what he was like, you don't have to tell me.

NELL. And he never mentioned you to me.

GABBY. It's not really something you tell your mum though, is it?

NELL. We weren't like a normal mother and son, we were extremely close. He wouldn't have been able to keep something like this from me, and he couldn't lie to save his life, so...

GABBY. So...? Sorry, so...you actually don't believe me?

(**NELL** *says nothing.*)

Oh my God...why would I come all the way over here to make something like this up?

NELL. Well, I don't know you, do I? You just landed in here and could be a psychopath for all I know. You could be someone who does this all the time, tricking vulnerable mothers with dead sons into giving you money.

(**GABBY** *is really taken aback by this.*)

GABBY. First of all, that would be a sociopathic thing to do not a psychopathic one and I'm neither of those things.

NELL. Good to know.

GABBY. And second of all, I'm not a complete idiot, even though you're treating me like one. And third of all...no offense, you don't seem that vulnerable.

NELL. My son would never have done something like this.

GABBY. Well, I'm telling you he did. And I'm sorry to be ruining your perfect memory of him, really I am, but it's not like I had a lot of other options. This is his mess as much as it is mine and since he's not around to deal with it...

NELL. You thought I'd be the next best thing?

GABBY. Well, sort of, yeah.

(**NELL** *sighs.*)

NELL. So...I presume you want some money or something?

GABBY. I'm not looking for cash off you.

NELL. Good because I don't have any.

GABBY. Yeah, obviously.

(*A beat.* **NELL** *looks at her.*)

NELL. What's that supposed to mean?

GABBY. Well, that you live here, and you're renting out rooms and...look, you're clearly not minted is all I meant, if I was looking for cash, I think I'd try someone else. Anyway, I don't need money, I've got a sweet part-time job in the deli near my house.

NELL. A deli?

GABBY. Yeah. I always work Sundays so it's time and a half.

NELL. What do your family think about all this?

GABBY. They don't know...you're actually the first person I've told.

NELL. That you're pregnant?

GABBY. Besides the doctor obviously but technically she told me.

NELL. You haven't told anyone else? What about your parents?

GABBY. No way. My mum would murder me. As in, I would literally be killed by my own mother.

NELL. I'm sure that's not true.

GABBY. She's been banging on about it my whole life. And she's so proud of me now, doing well in uni and that so...I'm not telling her. It would break her heart.

NELL. So where does she think you are now?

GABBY. Summer internship.

NELL. But you're not planning on staying here all summer?

>   *(A pause.)*

GABBY. Just until the baby comes.

NELL. Oh Jesus.

GABBY. Look I'm sorry but it was getting harder and harder to hide it behind baggy jumpers. Everyone was going to start noticing. I had to get out.

NELL. What about your friends? Couldn't you have stayed with them?

GABBY. Haven't told any of them. I didn't want them to think I'm, like, one of those girls who gets pregnant.

NELL. What kind of girl is that?

>   (**GABBY** *shrugs her shoulders.*)

GABBY. Dunno...just never thought I'd be one of them.

NELL. How did you keep it from everyone?

GABBY. Every day for the last two months I basically just sat in the library at a desk near the loo. My mates thought I was crazy studying with a bad UTI. We had our exams last week so no one was really up to much. Now they're all in Ayia Napa and I'm here in County Clare...

NELL. You sat your exams?

GABBY. Yeah, I couldn't miss them or I'd have to repeat the year. And I am not staying in uni longer than I need to, I want to get out and get a real job as soon as possible. That's why I couldn't get away until now. I just wanted to get them done with no stress.

NELL. No stress?

GABBY. As in drama. If my friends found out they would have known it was Robin's baby and then it would have all kicked off. I didn't want to do that to him.

NELL. They knew you were seeing each other?

GABBY. Two of my really close friends knew, yeah. So they can "corroborate my story" in a court of law if that's where you're going with this.

NELL. It wasn't but...

GABBY. But what?

NELL. Gabby. I don't know what planet you're living on but when your baby arrives you are going to need proper money to look after it. And you're going to need lots of support around you from your family and friends. Whether or not this is his baby you are about to become a single mother and you should start taking this more seriously.

GABBY. Oh, but I'm not keeping it.

NELL. What?

GABBY. I thought that was obvious?

NELL. Not really, no.

GABBY. I'm going to give it up for adoption. That's why I came here; *Ireland,* you know, seemed like a good place to give up a baby.

> (**NELL** *puts her head in her hands.*)

NELL. God, give me strength.

> (*A sharp knock coming from the door into the hallway.*)

(*Calling out.*) Come in!

(**CHERYL-ANN** *sticks her head around the doorway wearing nothing but a towel.*)

CHERYL-ANN. Hi there. Mel?

NELL. It's Nell.

CHERYL-ANN. Nell! Oh my gosh, I've been calling you *Mel* the whole time.

NELL. Not to worry.

CHERYL-ANN. Okay, Nell. (*Getting it into her head.*) Nell, Nell, Nell. Rhymes with bell.

GABBY. So does Mel?

NELL. What can I help you with, Cheryl-Ann?

CHERYL-ANN. My shower's cold. And my thyroid is all over the place and I really need a quick de-clam.

NELL. Have you turned on the red switch beside the door?

CHERYL-ANN. Red switch? Huh, I must have missed that.

NELL. That turns on the shower.

CHERYL-ANN. Gotcha.

NELL. This is all in the information sheet I gave you on arrival.

CHERYL-ANN. Funny, I didn't read that.

(*Awkward pause.*)

Alrighty, thanks for your help. Appreciate it.

NELL. No bother.

CHERYL-ANN. (*To* **GABBY**.) Hi there.

GABBY. Hey.

(**CHERYL-ANN** *leaves.* **GABBY** *looks at* **NELL**, *confused.*)

NELL. Airbnb. She arrived last night. I meant to block off this whole weekend but the feckin' app…

GABBY. You do Airbnb?

NELL. You're looking at a Superhost.

GABBY. Is that a good thing?

NELL. Apparently so.

GABBY. So people actually want to come here on holidays then?

NELL. Does that surprise you?

GABBY. Just very far away from anything, is all.

NELL. I think that's part of the appeal.

> (**GABBY** *looks unsure.*)

Look, Gabby, I feel for you, really I do, but this weekend is not a good time for this.

GABBY. Why because you have a weird Airbnb guest?

NELL. No. Because Orla is staying here this weekend.

> (*A beat.*)

GABBY. Orla? As in Orla, Orla?

NELL. Yes, she's arriving this afternoon. I had better keep an eye on my phone.

GABBY. Why's she coming here?

NELL. Because she's his wife. And tomorrow is his six-month anniversary.

GABBY. Shit…

NELL. Yes. Exactly.

> (*A silence.* **NELL** *has put on her glasses to check her phone. Sends Orla a text "How are you getting on?".*)

GABBY. How long is she staying?

NELL. Until Sunday.

GABBY. Well, it's all good because she doesn't know a thing about me and Robin.

NELL. It's "all good"?

GABBY. She wouldn't even recognise me, or know that I was a student of his. I could just be another Airbnb person.

NELL. No, no, no absolutely not, you're staying somewhere else.

GABBY. There's nowhere else around here?

NELL. There's plenty of places.

GABBY. But I've just come all this way. Please, Nell, I'm tired. You'll barely see me, I promise. I can stay put in one of the rooms and watch telly all weekend.

NELL. There are no tellies in any of the rooms.

GABBY. I'll go on my phone then.

NELL. The internet here is…intermittent at best.

GABBY. Oh my God, what is this place?

NELL. A friend of mine, Stevie, has a guesthouse in the village. It's lovely, much nicer than here.

GABBY. Sounds expensive.

NELL. We'll figure it out.

GABBY. And what am I supposed to do there all weekend?

NELL. I don't know. What were you planning on doing here?

(*A pause.* **GABBY** *doesn't really know.*)

You should have called me before making the journey over.

GABBY. I didn't have your number, did I? And this is hardly something that's great to chat about over the phone. I thought it would be more respectful this way.

NELL. Turning up out of nowhere?

>   (**GABBY** *is stung.*)

GABBY. I shouldn't have come here.

>   (*A pause.*)

NELL. Why did you?

GABBY. Because I thought you would get it. Robin told me about how you got pregnant with him when you were at uni and how it was an accident. He told me how much it messed up your life. That's why I thought you of all people would understand. I didn't expect you to be so...

NELL. He said that? That it messed up my life?

GABBY. Yeah.

NELL. That's not true. That's not true at all. He was the best thing, *is*, the best thing that ever happened...I can't believe he thought that. What did I say to make him think that?

GABBY. He didn't seem upset by it or anything just that it was a fact.

NELL. It's not a fact. It's not true.

GABBY. I must have got it wrong then.

NELL. Yes, you must have.

>   (*An awkward pause.* **GABBY** *knows she's messed up a bit.*)

What other things did he say?

GABBY. About what?

NELL. About me. About us.

GABBY. Eh, he told me that you did pottery? He always drank coffee out of your mugs.

NELL. Did he? Which ones?

GABBY. Eh, they were kind of beige, I think?

NELL. With a blue handle?

GABBY. Yeah. Could have been.

NELL. I gave them to him a few Christmases ago.

GABBY. Yeah, they were nice. He liked them.

NELL. Anything else? Anything else you remember he said?

GABBY. I mean, yeah, loads of stuff.

NELL. Like what?

GABBY. It wasn't anything he actually said but like, I could tell he really admired you. Like, the way he spoke about you, he clearly really loved you.

> (*This breaks* **NELL**. *She covers her mouth with her hand to stop herself from crying.*)

> (*Then a sudden rap on the door. It's* **CHERYL-ANN** *again, this time fully clothed. Door opens.*)

CHERYL-ANN. I'm not interrupting anything, am I?

NELL. (**NELL** *snapping out of it.*) No, we were just about to get going.

CHERYL-ANN. Nell, can I ask, is this area private or communal? Because in some places it's hard to tell.

NELL. It's...communal.

CHERYL-ANN. So, you don't mind if I make myself comfortable here later on?

NELL. Eh, no, of course not.

CHERYL-ANN. Mm, it's super toasty in here.

GABBY. You got your shower working then?

CHERYL-ANN. I did. It was wonderful. Oh and Nell, that body lotion? Delightful. I'll certainly be mentioning that in my review. I like to leave extensive reviews after all my stays.

NELL. Great...

CHERYL-ANN. It's the least I can do.

NELL. So do you have plans for the day?

CHERYL-ANN. Oh sure, I'm heading out to the Cliffs of Mo-Hair.

NELL. Ah, you'll love them. Spectacular.

GABBY. What are they?

NELL. I'll tell you later.

CHERYL-ANN. I'm really more interested in the bird species that inhabit the areas *around* the cliffs rather than the cliffs themselves. But I do hear the views are spectacular.

NELL. Well, have a lovely time.

CHERYL-ANN. Will do.

> (**NELL** *nods at her thinking she's going to leave now. A pause.* **CHERYL-ANN** *stays where she is.*)

This is slightly embarrassing, but didn't you say there'd be a self-service breakfast? I'm just wondering where that might –

NELL. Oh Jesus, the website says that doesn't it?

CHERYL-ANN. I double checked before I came down.

NELL. Eh...I have eggs?

CHERYL-ANN. I'm not really in an egg mood.

> (**NELL**'s *phone on the table pings loudly all of a sudden.* **NELL** *checks it. It's Orla. Panic.*)

NELL. Okay, how about this? Gabby you must be hungry too, right?

GABBY. Starving.

NELL. So why don't the two of you head down to Stevie's for breakfast together?

CHERYL-ANN. Fun. A breakfast buddy!

> (**GABBY** *glares at* **NELL**.)

NELL. Tell her I sent you and that I asked her to cook you the *full* full Irish, does that sound good? I'll pay, it's on me.

CHERYL-ANN. That's very generous. I wouldn't usually accept this, but I can hear my belly growling.

NELL. But you have to go now, okay? Cheryl-Ann you can drive Gabby down with you right?

CHERYL-ANN. Sure, I've got my rental.

NELL. Great. Right so, off ye go.

> (**GABBY** *doesn't move.*)

There are tellies in the rooms at Stevies and WiFi that actually works...

> (**GABBY** *still doesn't move.*)

Cheryl-Ann could you give us a minute?

CHERYL-ANN. Sure thing. I'll start the engine. Oh, and Nell, don't worry, I won't be putting this in my review.

(**NELL** *smiles at her. The minute* **CHERYL-
ANN** *leaves the room* **NELL***'s smile drops.*)

GABBY. You still don't believe me.

NELL. What?

GABBY. You don't believe me that this is Robin's baby.

NELL. I... I don't know. It's a lot to take in. What did you
expect?

GABBY. I didn't expect you to kick me out straight away.

NELL. I'm not kicking you out, I'm hiding you. It's different.

GABBY. Honestly, I thought you might be excited.

NELL. Excited?

GABBY. Well, yeah. It's your grandchild.

(*A pause.*)

NELL. My grandchild.

GABBY. I'll do a bloody paternity test thingy-ma-bob if
you want. But you can pay for it, not me. She's kicking
me now, doesn't want to leave.

NELL. It's a girl?

GABBY. Yeah. Poor thing. Do you want to feel her? She's
got a strong kick.

(**NELL** *stares at* **GABBY***'s belly a moment. But
her phone pings again snapping her out of it.*)

NELL. Please Gabby. You really have to leave now. We can
talk about this again, I promise, but you have go now.

GABBY. Alright, I'm going.

NELL. Thank you.

(**NELL** *helps* **GABBY** *get her things together,
ushering her out, pauses.*)

Don't you have a coat?

GABBY. No. It was summer in London.

NELL. You can't be going out in just that, here take mine.

> (**NELL** *helps* **GABBY** *put on her old, battered coat. A moment.*)

GABBY. Alright, well, bye then.

NELL. Bye.

GABBY. And good luck with Orla. Robin told me how you never got on.

NELL. What? Why would he tell you that?

GABBY. Because we spoke about stuff, about everything really.

NELL. Robin didn't know that.

> (**GABBY** *shrugs.*)

And we don't *not* get on. Orla is a very particular person. And she's been through a lot. We get on just fine.

> (**GABBY** *raises her eyebrows.*)

Go on, get out of here.

> (**GABBY** *leaves.*)

> (**NELL** *is alone in her grief again.*)

> (*The light changes a little, so does the weather. Maybe the sun peaks out briefly from behind a cloud or the rain turns from pattering and to drizzling... We're not sure how much time has passed until...*)

ORLA. (*Offstage.*) Nell? Hello?

> *(***NELL*** *snaps out of it. Puts on a face. She gets up to open the door, but* ***ORLA*** *has let herself in.)*

NELL. Orla. Hi.

ORLA. Sorry the door was open so I just –

NELL. Absolutely. Come in, come in.

> *(***ORLA*** *enters. Like* ***GABBY***, *she is carrying two bags – a large handbag and a travel case. Unlike* ***GABBY*** *her bags look sophisticated, as does her outfit.)*
>
> *(They embrace. Both of them trying to be warm but it's a bit formal, nonetheless.)*

ORLA. So good to see you.

NELL. You too. Sit down there. You made it in record time.

ORLA. Prebooked a taxi.

NELL. No better woman. Sorry the weather's dreadful.

ORLA. Not your fault.

NELL. Hopefully it'll clear a bit for tomorrow.

ORLA. Mmm. Bleak enough as it is.

> *(A pause.* ***ORLA*** *sits in the exact same spot* ***GABBY*** *was sitting in a while ago.)*

NELL. So, how have you been?

ORLA. Fine. You know, actually fine.

> *(Suddenly* ***ORLA****'s face crumples. She's trying to hold it together.)*

NELL. Oh, Orla.

ORLA. Sorry.

NELL. Please don't be. Can I get you something? How about a coffee?

ORLA. A coffee would be perfect.

> (**NELL** *busies herself with making a French press coffee for* **ORLA**.)

It's just been a long morning.

NELL. Tell me about it. How was the journey?

ORLA. It was fine. There was a bit of an incident when I got into Shannon.

NELL. What kind of incident?

ORLA. Just this horrible man at customs, he kept asking me questions about the ashes. It was awful.

NELL. Don't they have to ask questions if you're declaring something like that?

ORLA. It was his tone. His tone was so cold. He didn't have to use a tone like that.

NELL. Absolutely. No. You're right.

ORLA. I started crying, and he still kept *grilling* me. Like I was doing something illegal. You'd swear he'd never seen a woman carrying her husband's ashes before.

NELL. Where are they now?

ORLA. Here, in my bag. Do you want to see them?

NELL. Eh. No. No, later is fine.

> (*A pause.*)

Here's your coffee, love.

ORLA. Thank you.

NELL. I got it in the new fancy deli in town. Beans roasted in Galway, apparently. Thought you might like it.

ORLA. That's very thoughtful. Thank you.

(*A silence.*)

Do you think I should write a letter of complaint to the airport? That man shouldn't be in a customer facing role with an attitude like that.

NELL. If it would make you feel better...

ORLA. You must think I'm ridiculous.

NELL. I don't. It's tough being out there, the world is not made for grieving people.

ORLA. Have you been out much?

NELL. Only for the essentials.

ORLA. Have you seen much of Stevie or...anyone?

NELL. Not really, no. She calls but... Ah, I'm still not really up for much, to be honest.

ORLA. Fair. Where's Shep?

NELL. Had to put him down three weeks ago.

ORLA. Ah, no. Poor Shep.

NELL. He had a good stint. Fourteen years. That's ninety eight in dog years.

ORLA. Wow, imagine getting to ninety eight.

(*A beat.*)

NELL. It is quiet around here without him.

ORLA. Would you get a new dog? A puppy?

NELL. No need. The flock looks as if it's only getting smaller.

ORLA. But it would be company for you.

NELL. (*Brushing it off.*) Ah. No need for that either.

ORLA. Strange being here without him. Robin, I mean, not...

NELL. I suppose it's normal for me now. I wake up thinking he's still in London and then remembering...

ORLA. I know what you mean. Sometimes at work I pick up my phone to text him...

NELL. How has work been going?

ORLA. I'm taking more time off.

NELL. I thought you had gone back?

ORLA. I think it's been good, you know, to process everything. I'm feeling a lot of rage at the world right now. My therapist says it's normal. But it feels... overwhelming at times.

NELL. I'm glad you're seeing a therapist.

ORLA. It wasn't my decision. I have to go for work.

NELL. Are they paying for it?

ORLA. Yes, actually they are.

NELL. That's good of them.

ORLA. No, it's a stupid optics thing. There was this minor incident with a woman who was going on maternity leave and she thought I was...sorry, to be clear, it was bullshit, the woman was completely deluded. But the word "bullying" was used and she felt I was...actually I don't want to talk about it because it wasn't even true. But anyway, now I have to see this therapist, so everyone thinks I'm, whatever, *complying*. Anyway, yes, *rage*. Apparently, it's a common side effect of grief.

NELL. So I've heard.

ORLA. You know, I don't think I'm asking too much to just be happy? To have my husband here. To have a family like everyone else seems to have. I don't think I'm asking for too much, do you?

NELL. No. Of course not.

ORLA. Ugh, sorry, listen to me, going on and on and there's you... I can't imagine what it's been like to lose your only child.

NELL. I think you can imagine, all too well.

ORLA. Yeah, well, lots of people don't see it that way.

NELL. Lots of people haven't suffered like you have.

(Pause.)

ORLA. Thank you for always sending beautiful cards.

NELL. They won't help you feel any better but sometimes it's all you can do.

ORLA. No, I appreciated that you always marked it. I always planted a tree. I visited them the weekend after he died.

NELL. How were they?

ORLA. They were trees! Now that's all I have; four fucking trees in an eco-forest up in Lancashire.

NELL. Even in the depths of your grief, it is beautiful in a way, that you've given something back to the world.

ORLA. I don't care about the world! I care about...

NELL. What?

> (**ORLA** *takes a deep breath...in through the nose [she doesn't get to out through the mouth] ...)*

ORLA. I need to talk to you about something important.

NELL. Okay.

ORLA. Okay. Okay... So, you know how we had been doing IVF? And it hadn't been working.

NELL. Yes, I know. Robin was devastated for you.

ORLA. And we were planning on trying again.

NELL. Yes, he told me that too.

ORLA. So we don't have any embryos left but we do have frozen samples that Robin had deposited a few years ago.

NELL. Right.

ORLA. His semen.

NELL. I'm following.

ORLA. So I want to continue our plan and try again to have our baby.

(*A pause.*)

NELL. Without him?

ORLA. I don't see any reason why I shouldn't keep trying.

NELL. I thought they said your womb wasn't...

(*A horrible silence.* **ORLA** *doesn't help her find the word...*)

ORLA. I want you to know I am not making this decision lightly. I have been thinking about it non-stop for the last six months.

NELL. So are you asking me if I think you should do this or telling me you are?

(**ORLA** *isn't really sure herself.*)

ORLA. I can't talk to Robin about it and you're the closest thing I have to him now so... I guess I am asking you what you think, yes. What do you think?

NELL. Orla, the last time you tried, Robin said you didn't have an easy ride after it didn't work out.

ORLA. Well, it's very different this time.

NELL. Different how?

ORLA. I'm in a different place. I've a different mindset. I've met this woman.

NELL. A woman?

ORLA. This kind of spiritual guidance type woman. A friend recommended her. Please don't laugh –

NELL. I'm not.

ORLA. Because she's been helping me a lot.

NELL. Okay. That's good... How? If you don't mind me asking?

ORLA. She puts her hands in different places on my body and she has these cards that...you know, it doesn't really matter how she's helping me what matters is that I feel in a really settled place with all that stuff now.

NELL. What stuff?

ORLA. My fertility.

NELL. Oh. Really?

ORLA. Yes. And she says that's the most important thing. To feel ready to welcome a baby.

NELL. Okay...

ORLA. Positive thoughts will help my body during the process.

NELL. Does your therapist know about any of this?

ORLA. God, no. I don't tell him anything that's actually real.

NELL. Right. Orla, this is a huge thing to face into on your own.

ORLA. A lot of other women have done it alone. You included.

NELL. Sure, but have they just lost their husbands? What is it they say "no big changes within the first year".

ORLA. Oh Nell, I'm sorry but fuck that. Sorry but, seriously. I mean who came up with those rules?

NELL. I don't know. Just something I've heard.

ORLA. Exactly. I mean, sure, if I had all the time in the world, of course I'd wait. The only reason I'm doing this now is because I am running out of time and what is the point in waiting when I know I want it. I want it more than anything.

NELL. Have you been speaking to anyone else? Your doctor? Your mother?

ORLA. She didn't think I should try again after the first time. I've spoken to the fertility clinic, and they said it's completely my decision, I can start the process anytime I like. This could be your grandchild, Nell. Wouldn't that be special?

(**NELL** *is at a loss.*)

NELL. I don't know what you want me to say here, Orla.

(*A pause.*)

ORLA. I want you to say that you think it's a great idea and you think everything is going to be fine.

NELL. I can't tell you that.

ORLA. No... No one can it seems. I know it sounds ridiculous but since he died I've had this feeling. This really strong feeling that I will have a baby. That all these years of sadness and trying so desperately to be happy are going to *mean* something. They have to, right?

(**NELL** *says nothing.*)

(*A sound of the front door opening and someone coming into the house.*)

You have guests?

NELL. Guest. Just one American. She shouldn't be too much trouble.

ORLA. Oh.

NELL. I know I wanted the place to ourselves but I mixed up the dates on the app. I'll try get rid of her fast.

(*But it's* **GABBY** *who enters the room, sheepishly.*)

GABBY. Hiya.

NELL. What are you doing here?

GABBY. Stevie's had a flood last night so there's no rooms at the inn. Literally.

NELL. I told her to get that bloody roof fixed.

ORLA. Hi?

GABBY. Hi...

ORLA. You're not American.

GABBY. Eh, no.

NELL. Orla this is an old friend of my friend, Stevie. She's Stevie's friend's daughter. From England. Distant friends. She was going to stay here tonight but then she wanted to stay in the village instead so I thought Stevie's would be better... (*To* **GABBY**.) Why don't you wait in the hall and I'll call the Seafront Hotel?

GABBY. Yeah, sure.

ORLA. Why can't she just stay here?

> (**GABBY** *pauses at the door, conflicted.*)

NELL. Because...the Seafront is more central.

ORLA. To where?

GABBY. I love the Seafront Hotel.

ORLA. Have you been there since the new owners? It's a dump. Is that...do you have the same coat?

NELL. She was very cold earlier on, I said she could borrow it.

> (**GABBY** *looks at* **NELL**, *this isn't a lie, she nods in agreement.*)

ORLA. Ah Nell, you can't let a pregnant girl stay in that kip. She should stay here.

NELL. No really Orla, it's Robin's anniversary, I wanted the place to ourselves.

ORLA. Sure there's another guest here already?

NELL. Yes, but she'll be no trouble.

GABBY. Neither will I, I promise.

> (**NELL** *can't find another reason to shut her down.*)

NELL. Alright. The barn is empty, why don't you head there right now?

GABBY. A barn?

NELL. It's renovated.

ORLA. The barn is tiny. You take my room. Nell, I presume I'm in the attic as usual?

NELL. Eh, yes, it's all set up.

ORLA. *(To* **GABBY**.*)* The attic is much cosier and there's a bath.

GABBY. No honestly, I couldn't, the barn sounds fine.

ORLA. Not at all. I'll show you up there myself.

NELL. No, no, I'm the host! I'll show her.

ORLA. Don't be silly, you've plenty to do. Here give me your bag.

> (**GABBY** *open-mouthed hands* **ORLA** *her rucksack.* **NELL** *can't think of what to say to stop this so is standing, useless.*)

So how far along are you?

GABBY. Seven months.

ORLA. You shouldn't be trapsing around outside especially in your condition. Sorry, what did you say your name was?

GABBY. Gabby.

ORLA. Gabby. Gorgeous name. So nice to meet you. I'm Orla.

NELL. Robin's wife.

End of Part One

PART TWO

(The same day but later in the afternoon. It's still a drizzly, grey and miserable summer's day.)

*(A cosy fire has been lit. **NELL** is by the window in the living room and **ORLA** is sitting by the fire with a book, trying to ignore **CHERYL-ANN** who is also sitting nearby.)*

CHERYL-ANN. If I had to pick my favourite bird, I would say...the Meadow Pipet.

ORLA. Can't say I'm familiar with it.

CHERYL-ANN. Nell, you gotta know it.

NELL. I do.

CHERYL-ANN. Wait, favourite house bird or wild bird?

(Pause.)

ORLA. You asked yourself the question.

CHERYL-ANN. Because house bird would have to be a Cockatiel. I have five at home; Melvin, Judas, Herb, Henrietta and Michael. Very sweet little guys. Monica is looking after them while I'm away.

ORLA. *(Obviously doesn't know or care who Monica is.)* That's nice...

CHERYL-ANN. She's my neighbour. Very old lady. A tonne of ailments.

NELL. Weren't you about to head out for a walk, Cheryl-Ann?

CHERYL-ANN. Just waiting for that rain to pass.

NELL. It's only a light drizzle at this stage.

ORLA. Sometimes walking in the rain can be invigorating.

CHERYL-ANN. I couldn't agree more. And you know what rain means?

> *(She waits...neither of them knows where she's going with this...)*

Rainbows!

> *(**NELL** suddenly spots something outside.)*

NELL. Feck it anyway, the fence is down. I'll have to head out before they notice. You'll be alright here?

ORLA. Perfect. Can I do anything to help?

NELL. No, no, I'll be back shortly just don't...stay put. Okay?

> *(**NELL** throws on her coat and boots and heads out the back door into the weather.)*

CHERYL-ANN. Wow. Real life farming in action.

> *(**ORLA** smiles at her but goes back to her book in an effort not to engage.)*

I take it you're not that interested in birds then?

ORLA. Not particularly, no.

CHERYL-ANN. Haven't you ever watched a murmuration of starlings move and sway together at sunset and thought *(places hand on heart)*, my God, it's good to be alive.

ORLA. Not really, no.

CHERYL-ANN. Well, next time you see one, you'll know what I mean. There are also so many beautiful species in this area. A lot of which won't be around much longer.

ORLA. I'm more of a dog person.

CHERYL-ANN. People love dogs. But contrary to popular belief, birds are much more similar to humans than dogs are.

ORLA. *(Non-committal.)* Mmm.

CHERYL-ANN. Think about it; they build homes, they raise families, they go on vacation. And of course, they love to sing.

ORLA. Not all humans love to sing.

CHERYL-ANN. Oh yes, they do.

ORLA. I don't.

CHERYL-ANN. Huh. There is nothing better in this world to ease the soul than singing.

ORLA. Peace and quiet? That really eases my soul.

CHERYL-ANN. And birds can do what we all wish we could do; *fly.* Nine point nine times out of ten, when you ask someone what they'd like to be reincarnated as they say a bird so they can fly.

ORLA. Do you ask people that often?

CHERYL-ANN. It tells you a lot about a person.

> *(A moment.* **CHERYL-ANN** *is weighing up what she thinks* **ORLA** *might be...)*

ORLA. I'm going to get some reading done now. If you don't mind?

CHERYL-ANN. Great idea. In fact, I have some reading of my own here...

> (**CHERYL-ANN** *takes out a small book.)*

It's a pocket guide of all the bird species in Ireland. I've made a list of the ones I want to spot on this trip. All of which are on the red list. So sad.

ORLA. Mmm.

CHERYL-ANN. You know that means that they're going to be extinct soon?

ORLA. I didn't know that, no.

CHERYL-ANN. By soon, I mean in the next hundred years. Do you want to hear some?

> (**ORLA** *opens her mouth to say a firm no, but*
> **CHERYL-ANN** *continues first.*)

Okay, still to spot; Cormorant, European Storm Petrel, Peregrine Falcon, Eurasian Bittern, Marsh Harrier, Sparrowhawk, Curlew, Yellow-legged Herring Gull, Stonechat, Dunnock –

> (**ORLA** *puts down her book, annoyed, just as*
> **GABBY** *sticks her head around the door. She*
> *is wearing a borrowed dressing gown and her*
> *wet hair is in a towel.* **ORLA** *is relieved she*
> *has been saved from listening to a bird list.)*

ORLA. Hi!

GABBY. Sorry, I thought I heard people leaving.

ORLA. That was Nell, she's gone to fix a fence.

GABBY. I was going to make a cup of tea, but I'll come back later.

ORLA. Don't be silly, come in! Come in, please.

CHERYL-ANN. This is the communal area after all.

GABBY. I don't want to disturb you.

ORLA. You're *really* not disturbing anything.

CHERYL-ANN. We were talking about reincarnation.

ORLA. Please come in. Look, warm up there. I'll make you a tea.

> (**ORLA** *has already gotten up off the couch*
> *and is moving around boiling the kettle,*

getting a mug, etc. **GABBY** *hesitantly comes into the room properly.)*

CHERYL-ANN. Gabby. If you could come back as any kind of creature, what would it be?

GABBY. Like, from the dead?

CHERYL-ANN. Yeah.

GABBY. I'm not really into stuff like that.

CHERYL-ANN. Stuff like what?

GABBY. Like, spooky stuff, magic or whatever.

CHERYL-ANN. *(Slightly taken aback.)* Huh. What about Harry Potter?

GABBY. Ew. No.

CHERYL-ANN. Everyone likes Harry Potter.

GABBY. Haven't read it.

CHERYL-ANN. But you're from London?

GABBY. So?

CHERYL-ANN. That's where – oh my God, you gotta read it. Look *(Referencing her sweater.)* Expecto Patronum.

GABBY. Yeah, I don't know what that means.

CHERYL-ANN. It's a spell that conjures your Patronus; a kind of ghostly animal that protects you in a time of need, everyone in the magical community has one.

GABBY. That sounds...kind of weird.

CHERYL-ANN. You have *got* to read the books. Then you can do a quiz online to find out what animal your Patronus would be. It's pretty fun.

ORLA. I'm guessing yours was some kind of bird?

CHERYL-ANN. Unfortunately, no. Mine was a skunk.

*(If possible, **GABBY** and **ORLA** meet each other's eye here and try not to laugh.)*

GABBY. I see you as more of a Puffin.

CHERYL-ANN. I take that as a huge compliment. Puffins are highly intelligent creatures. Sadly, in decline. *(Sad for a moment then to **GABBY**.)* I can send you the link to the quiz if you like? Now that I got you on Instagram.

GABBY. Eh, yeah, sure.

CHERYL-ANN. Ooh, or we could do it together tonight? What are you guys thinking in terms of dinner? I'm going to this traditional Irish bar called Mulligans. They do world famous fish and chips, apparently.

GABBY. I think I'm taking it easy, I need to rest cos of… *(She pats her belly.)*.

ORLA. Yeah, Nell and I are planning a quiet night too.

CHERYL-ANN. Oh sure, I totally get that. Quiet nights all round then. Good… Good.

ORLA. Any tea in particular, Gabby?

GABBY. Just normal is fine.

CHERYL-ANN. I'd love a mint.

ORLA. Weren't you about to head out?

CHERYL-ANN. Oh jeez, I almost forgot. All this riveting conversation. It's my favourite part of foreign travel; getting to know complete strangers.

(Both of them smile politely at her.)

Anyway ladies, I'm going to walk down the road a little and scout the area. I'm hoping to spot a Curlew.

(No one says anything.)

Well, wish me luck. Might be the last chance I have to see one.

ORLA. Good luck.

GABBY. Good luck.

> *(And with that,* **CHERYL-ANN** *has finally left the building.)*

ORLA. So...she's a friend of yours?

GABBY. Fuck, no. She's a complete stranger, had to have breakfast with her this morning.

ORLA. Oh God, why was that?

GABBY. Just, not enough tables.

ORLA. Honestly, the nutters that pass through this place. I don't know how Nell does it.

GABBY. Why does she do it?

> *(***ORLA** *has made the tea.)*

ORLA. Needs the money, I suppose. Here's your tea, darling, and a sneaky biscuit.

GABBY. Thank you, really very kind of you.

> *(***GABBY** *starts to go back to her room.)*

ORLA. Where are you going?

GABBY. I can take it back up to the room.

ORLA. Don't be silly. Sit down. Enjoy the warmth.

GABBY. I don't want to be in your space.

ORLA. You saw who was just in my space? You're a relief. Honestly.

GABBY. Alright...just for a minute. It is much warmer down here.

> *(***GABBY** *settles into a comfortable spot by the fire.)*

ORLA. It's good to stay warm when you're feeling ropey.

GABBY. Is it that obvious?

ORLA. You look a bit pale.

GABBY. Stress of the journey, is all. I'm sure I'll be fine.

ORLA. So, you only arrived today?

GABBY. This morning, yeah.

ORLA. And you're over visiting Stevie?

GABBY. Who?

ORLA. Stevie? I thought –

GABBY. Yes! Yeah, I thought it would be nice to get away for a bit. A holiday.

ORLA. People love coming here on holidays, I never got it. But I suppose when you grow up somewhere it's different.

GABBY. So you're from here too then?

ORLA. A town close by, yeah. I moved to London to get away from home and ended up marrying someone from down the road. Typical.

GABBY. Yeah, typical.

ORLA. Where do you live?

GABBY. Eh, London too. Lewisham.

ORLA. Oh yeah, I know Lewisham a bit. My husband actually worked close by in the University of Greenwich.

GABBY. Yeah, yeah, that's nearby.

(*A pause.*)

What about you? Where do you live?

ORLA. Islington. Right by Highbury Fields.

GABBY. That area is like, the dream.

ORLA. I know, right? I promised myself when I was earning enough, I would buy there. And so I did.

GABBY. That's so cool.

ORLA. But it's horrifically posh to be honest. My husband always hated it... He thought it was all middle-class couples with fancy buggies. He was right.

(A silence.)

GABBY. I'm really sorry for your loss, by the way. Nell told me what happened...

ORLA. Thank you, honey.

GABBY. Can't imagine how awful it must be to lose your partner.

ORLA. It is, awful... Sorry, I still don't really know what to say when people sympathise.

GABBY. You don't have to say anything.

(A pause.)

It's hard to believe it. As in, that someone can just be gone.

ORLA. I know exactly what you mean. I keep thinking he's going to show up and this will all be over.

GABBY. Yeah, I get that.

ORLA. Have you ever lost someone close to you?

GABBY. Not really. Like my Nan, but I was really young so I didn't really get it. Not anyone that I actually missed day to day, if that's not too bad a thing to say.

ORLA. No, I get you.

GABBY. Nell said you're scattering his ashes tomorrow?

ORLA. Yes. She wanted to make a bit of a thing of it.

GABBY. Sounds nice. Sorry not nice but, you know.

ORLA. Yeah, I think it's important for her. The funeral was... I can't even really remember it. We were both still in complete shock.

GABBY. That's fair.

ORLA. And I also completely fucked it up.

GABBY. How?

ORLA. Ugh, it doesn't matter now.

(*A pause.*)

Sorry, I'm not great company at the moment. It's hard not to get sucked into the grief chat spiral.

GABBY. I don't mind, honestly.

ORLA. So, distract me, what are you going to get up to while you're here?

GABBY. Oh just, chilling really. I thought some fresh air would be good for the baby.

ORLA. And how are you finding it?

GABBY. Being pregnant?

ORLA. Yeah.

GABBY. Eh... At the start, I didn't really feel much.

ORLA. Wow, lucky.

GABBY. But in the last few weeks it's been getting really uncomfortable. Also, I know this is bad to say but like it's just so boring. My friends are all in Ayia Napa right now. I can't wait to just get it out and feel like myself again to be honest.

ORLA. When's your due date?

GABBY. August.

ORLA. That'll fly.

GABBY. Hopefully. I want it to come quickly but also, I'm dreading it. For something that's been happening since we literally existed, I don't know how they haven't found an easier way of getting it out. Like a zip, or something.

ORLA. Have you thought about a C-Section?

GABBY. I watched a video of someone having one last night.

ORLA. Oh no. Don't do that.

GABBY. Freaked the shit out of me, not gonna lie.

ORLA. A midwife told me this once; it is one of the most natural things in the world, millions of women have done it before you and millions will do it again. So, that can't be too bad, right?

GABBY. You seem to know more about it than I do.

ORLA. Well, I have been pregnant a few times.

GABBY. Seriously?

ORLA. Yeah.

GABBY. How many times?

ORLA. Four. Well, four officially. But none of them went to term. Three miscarriages.

GABBY. Oh my God.

ORLA. And one emergency C-Section at twenty four weeks.

GABBY. Oh fuck...

ORLA. Sorry have I shocked you?

GABBY. Yeah. No! No, I just had no idea.

ORLA. Well, how would you? Probably half the women you see walking down the street have had some kind of pregnancy trauma. Maybe more.

GABBY. I am so, so sorry that that all happened to you. It sounds horrific.

ORLA. I'm not telling you any of this to scare you, by the way. I was very unlucky. Your baby is going to be perfect. You're young and that makes it much easier.

GABBY. I don't know what to say, I'm just so sorry. And here's me complaining about this big bump and I had no idea.

ORLA. Not at all. It's better for me to talk about it openly. I hope you don't feel uncomfortable about me bringing it up?

GABBY. Of course not.

ORLA. Because some people, friends of mine, do find it uncomfortable. But I feel like, "oh sorry, did I make *you* feel uncomfortable? Think about how I feel having to live with it every day of my life." You know?

GABBY. You're so right.

ORLA. Because it happened. It has happened to me. And if I can't talk about it, something real, then what is the point in talking at all?

GABBY. Agreed.

ORLA. There's so much secrecy and shame around pregnancy still, don't you think?

GABBY. I don't know. I haven't really spoken to anyone about it.

ORLA. What?

GABBY. My family don't know I'm pregnant.

(*Beat.* **ORLA** *takes this in.*)

ORLA. Well, that proves my point.

GABBY. I suppose.

ORLA. So, your parents don't know?

GABBY. No.

ORLA. You don't live with them then?

GABBY. I actually do most of the time, but I've got three mental younger brothers so they kind of keep my mum and stepdad pretty preoccupied. And then when I got bigger I was spending a lot of time in my auntie's flat. She's been away a lot since she met this Turkish dude, and she has this cat that I look after, Hamish. She pays me for feeding him too, so staying there is like the easiest cash ever.

ORLA. Would you think of talking to your mum about it?

GABBY. That's the last thing I'd do.

ORLA. Why's that?

GABBY. See, she had me when she was at school. And I think it kind of messed her up. Not that she regrets it but...she might regret it a bit. Not me, she loves me, but...she was really clever. And she had to start work instead of sitting her A levels so yeah...this is literally her worst nightmare for me. That's why I want to sort it out on my own. So, she doesn't need to know anything about it.

ORLA. But when the baby arrives...won't she need to know then?

GABBY. I'm not planning on keeping it.

  (*A beat.*)

ORLA. Oh, okay.

GABBY. Do you think I'm a bad person?

ORLA. No! And I would never judge any woman on her decisions. Ever. And this is *so* none of my business what you do with your baby so...if it feels right for you, you should do it.

(They smile at each other. A silence.)

GABBY. What are you thinking?

ORLA. I'm thinking about how we spend all our twenties trying not to get pregnant and then most of our thirties desperately trying to do the exact opposite. And it sucks.

GABBY. Yeah. Totally.

ORLA. I knew this girl, who got pregnant by accident when she was around your age with this complete waste of space. I mean, he was a nightmare, he would have been a terrible partner. So she had an abortion and it was the absolute right thing to do at the time...but I think sometimes she wonders if...

GABBY. What?

ORLA. See, she really wants to have a baby now. And it's painful to think that it was so easy then and so much more difficult now.

GABBY. Do you think I'm going to regret it?

ORLA. No! That's not what I'm saying, what am I trying to say? That we can only do our best, I suppose. Our best at the time with our circumstances and...oh, who the fuck knows! Don't listen to me!

*(**GABBY** laughs. She really likes **ORLA**.)*

I'm sure people have been giving you all kinds of advice so I don't want to add to the pile.

GABBY. Well, not really because I haven't actually told anyone.

ORLA. You know, Nell was pregnant with Robin when she was around your age. So she'd probably be a good person to talk to about it, if you wanted to.

(A pause.)

What about the father? Not to sound conventional but I presume there was one.

GABBY. Yeah, he's not really in the picture anymore...

ORLA. "Not in the picture" as in you broke up or he legged it after you told him?

GABBY. Eh, yeah, he broke up with me.

ORLA. What a coward.

GABBY. No, it wasn't like that. He was a decent guy really. Just all got a bit real.

ORLA. Well, it's very real for you too but you've no choice, do you?

GABBY. Honestly, he wasn't a bad guy...it just got a bit complicated.

(*A beat.* **GABBY** *continues, cautiously.*)

He had a wife, you see.

(*Pause.* **ORLA** *takes this in.*)

ORLA. Oh.

GABBY. Yeah...

ORLA. Did you know that?

GABBY. Yeah, I did.

(*Another pause.*)

Bet you think I'm a bad person now.

ORLA. No. No, I don't judge people like that. Anyway, the responsibility rests on him, he's the one who is married.

GABBY. I honestly do not know what I was thinking now. I wish I could go back in time and stop myself, you know? Like, it didn't feel that bad a thing to do at the time but now... I feel really, really awful about it. I do.

ORLA. Look everyone makes mistakes. And you're still so young.

GABBY. I don't feel that young.

ORLA. I presume he was a fair bit older than you if he was married?

(**GABBY** *nods.*)

Then he should know better.

GABBY. I just feel so guilty because his wife...it turns out she's actually a really cool person.

ORLA. Well, maybe you could apologise to her?

GABBY. Seriously?

ORLA. If it would make you feel better, sure. And you'd be doing her a favour; saving her from wasting years of her life married to a cheater. Because I'm telling you now; if they do it once, they'll do it again.

GABBY. I don't think he'll be doing it again.

ORLA. Trust me, he will. What was his name?

GABBY. Oh, eh, (*Panicking.*) Jez.

ORLA. Jez! Ugh. If you ever need someone to scratch his car you let me know...

(**GABBY** *laughs but* **ORLA** *means it.*)

I'm serious I've done it before. Honestly, why can't men handle real life? It pisses me off.

(*A pause.*)

GABBY. What happened to Robin's Dad?

ORLA. Nothing happened. He never knew him. Apparently, he was German or something? A tourist who Nell spent the night with but never saw again.

GABBY. Woah. And she was slut shaming me.

ORLA. She was, what?

GABBY. No, nothing, just, I didn't expect that.

ORLA. I know, dark horse.

*(They hear the back door open. **NELL** is coming back in.)*

Don't tell her I told you that by the way.

GABBY. I won't say anything, promise.

*(**NELL** blusters in from fixing the fence. She is distracted then clocks them both in the room.)*

NELL. Oh. You're both here?

ORLA. I made Gabby a cup of tea.

NELL. I can see that.

GABBY. She offered. I didn't ask her to.

ORLA. We were having a chat.

NELL. About what?

ORLA. Everything. Men, babies. How's the fence?

NELL. Gabby, shouldn't you be resting? Upstairs?

ORLA. She's resting here, it's probably freezing upstairs.

NELL. I'll make you a jar. You can go back to bed.

GABBY. Yeah. Sorry.

NELL. Go back to bed, as in, now. I'll bring it up to you.

*(**NELL** flicks the kettle on and finds a hot water bottle. **GABBY** gets up from the couch.)*

GABBY. *(To **ORLA**.)* Thanks for the tea.

ORLA. Anytime.

(**NELL** *is watching them, warily.* **GABBY** *is about to leave then something stops her. Probably her conscience.*)

GABBY. Can I just say, you're really nice.

ORLA. Oh. Thanks, honey.

GABBY. Like, really, really nice.

ORLA. You caught me on a good day. Honestly, I'm a complete bitch most of the time.

(**GABBY** *laughs and goes to leave but again stops at the door.*)

GABBY. Maybe that friend of yours, the one who can't get pregnant, maybe she will have a baby some day?

ORLA. I hope so, it would make her very happy.

(*A moment between them.* **GABBY** *leaves.*)

NELL. What was that about?

ORLA. We were talking about fertility.

NELL. Right...anything in particular?

ORLA. Did you know she hasn't told her family she's pregnant?

NELL. I did know that, yes.

ORLA. And her boyfriend dumped her when he found out.

(*A beat.*)

NELL. I didn't know that.

ORLA. You know, sometimes you feel as if you're the only person who is really alone and then you meet someone like her. I feel so sorry for her.

NELL. I wouldn't.

ORLA. Why's that?

NELL. She seems like she's got it under control.

> *(A pause.)*

Could I see them now?

ORLA. The ashes? Sure. They're right here...

> **(ORLA** *takes them out of her carry bag. She
> places them in front of* **NELL.** *A moment.)*

NELL. Actually, can you take them away? Take them away.

ORLA. Sure, where should I (put them)?

NELL. Just anywhere I can't see them. Please.

> **(ORLA** *finds an easy spot, maybe underneath
> the coffee table, out of sight but still near.)*

Thank you. Sorry. I can't...

ORLA. I know.

> *(A pause.* **ORLA** *takes a breath.)*

I'm sorry about the funeral.

> **(NELL** *looks at her, surprised.)*

I know I was being difficult. I wasn't thinking straight.

> **(NELL** *softens.)*

NELL. What does it matter now, I suppose? We were both
going out of our minds.

ORLA. Yeah. Still... I wish I could go back and let you say
the eulogy instead. You would have done a much better
job of it, at least.

NELL. It's fine, Orla. It's done. No point going over it again
now.

> *(A pause.)*

ORLA. I feel bad we never did this before.

NELL. Did what?

ORLA. Spent time like this, just the two of us.

NELL. Don't feel bad on my account.

ORLA. Every time we came home, I felt I had to see my family too and you know, it's hard to split the time.

NELL. Really, it never bothered me. Sure, I loved having him to myself whenever he came home.

ORLA. I guess I got that feeling too.

NELL. What feeling?

ORLA. Well, that you never really...

>　(**ORLA** *looks at* **NELL**, *she is unsure if she should say this, but she does...*)

Look, this is a bit awkward, but I always had the feeling that you never really liked me.

>　(*A beat.*)

NELL. Liked you? I, I don't know what to say to that.

ORLA. Robin was always telling me I was imagining it.

NELL. Yes, yes, you must have been.

ORLA. It's completely fine if you didn't, by the way. Don't.

NELL. It's not fine! I did. I do. Of course, I do.

ORLA. I know we were very different, Robin and I, but we loved each other.

NELL. I know you did.

ORLA. I always had this feeling that you thought he should have been with someone more... I don't know, creative. Or, free spirited.

NELL. You're very creative, with all your interior design bits...

ORLA. You know what I mean...

NELL. And as far as I can tell you were an extremely good influence on Robin. You're the only reason he finished the bloody PHD.

ORLA. I would have to agree with that.

NELL. God love him, he could be terribly laid back.

ORLA. Yes...

NELL. Which you aren't. So that was good.

ORLA. I'm...no.

NELL. You evened each other out, is what I'm saying.

ORLA. Sure.

NELL. And he settled down with you and got a mortgage and a proper job. I never saw him doing that.

ORLA. Really? I mean, isn't that what most people do?

NELL. I remember calling him one day and the two of you were in...what's that homeware place called?

        (**ORLA**'s *face lights up.*)

ORLA. Habitat?

NELL. Habitat! Hilarious to think of him in there.

ORLA. He hated it there.

NELL. Yes, I think you were fighting when he answered the phone.

ORLA. Probably.

NELL. It's normal to fight. Especially in somewhere like Habitat.

ORLA. All the fights we had over ridiculous things. When I think about how good to me he was and everything I put him through. I was feeling so desperate, you know, so sad after Lily... And he was so attentive. Especially, in the last six months before he died. He was really there for me, asking how I was coping, cooking me my favourite dinners, really looking after me. I feel so guilty I wasn't with him when it happened. I was supposed to look after him too, you know? I was his wife.

NELL. Orla. You really have nothing to feel guilty about... I've been thinking about what you asked me. About the IVF. And as much as I think it will be painful for you if it doesn't work out... I think Robin would want you to be happy. So, if you think that would make you happy, then why not try it at least.

ORLA. Oh, Nell. Thank you. Thank you for saying that.

NELL. I'm going to take this hot water bottle to Gabby. Then maybe you and I should go for a walk?

ORLA. Yeah, sounds good.

NELL. A quick one now, nothing too strenuous. This weekend was supposed to be healing for us both.

(**ORLA** *laughs at this.*)

You're going to get through this, Orla. You're stronger than you think.

(**NELL** *opens the door to go upstairs to* **GABBY**. **CHERYL-ANN** *is standing right there.*)

CHERYL-ANN. Hi there.

NELL. You're back already.

CHERYL-ANN. I certainly am.

NELL. *(Apologetically to* **ORLA**.*)* I'll be back in a second.

*(**NELL** leaves. **CHERYL-ANN** comes into the room.)*

CHERYL-ANN. You'll never guess what.

ORLA. What?

CHERYL-ANN. I saw one.

ORLA. One what?

CHERYL-ANN. One Curlew. It was so beautiful. A spot like that, it really puts you in a good mood, you know?

ORLA. That's great. I'm delighted for you.

CHERYL-ANN. You know, once you start noticing birds then everywhere you go; there they'll be, keeping you company. Unlike boring old humans who are so inhibited, so weighed down by everything. Birds don't worry about their future or regret their twenties; they don't dwell on what they don't have or beat themselves up about a particularly problematic relationship they keep returning to. They live in the moment. It's inspiring.

ORLA. Hm.

CHERYL-ANN. And you know what another cool thing is? They look out for each other. That's just a fact. And many of them even partner for life. Once they've found each other that's it. Unlike us muggles, am I right?

ORLA. Eh, I guess so.

CHERYL-ANN. That reminds me, how was your chat with Gabby?

ORLA. It was really nice. She's an amazing girl.

CHERYL-ANN. Wow. You think?

ORLA. Doing that all alone…it's really admirable.

CHERYL-ANN. Huh, I gotta say I was surprised to see the two of you together.

ORLA. Why's that?

CHERYL-ANN. Well, it's very big of you, that's all.

ORLA. What do you mean?

CHERYL-ANN. I guess, if she'd slept with my husband, I'd find it hard to look her in the eye, let alone make her a hot drink. I'm impressed.

ORLA. Excuse me?

CHERYL-ANN. Robin, right? Nell's son? Wasn't he your...?

ORLA. Husband. Yes.

CHERYL-ANN. Oh, and...oh.

(*It dawns on* **CHERYL-ANN** *she has really put her foot in it.*)

ORLA. What are you talking about?

CHERYL-ANN. I... I'm not sure now. Maybe never mind.

ORLA. That is an incredibly upsetting thing to say.

(**NELL** *comes back into the room. Senses the tension.*)

CHERYL-ANN. I really did not mean to upset you.

NELL. What's going on?

ORLA. Well, you have. Very much.

CHERYL-ANN. Oh gosh, I feel awful. I must have got my wires crossed somewhere.

NELL. What's she talking about?

ORLA. Cheryl-Ann accused that girl, Gabby, of sleeping with Robin.

NELL. What? That's crazy. That's, that's completely insane.

ORLA. Why would you even say that?

NELL. Yes, Cheryl-Ann. What is wrong with you?

CHERYL-ANN. I thought it all must be water under the bridge cos you two were sitting here chatting, I... I'm very sorry.

NELL. Where did you even get that idea from?

CHERYL-ANN. She told me.

>   (*A beat.*)

ORLA. Who did?

CHERYL-ANN. Gabby. When we were having breakfast this morning.

NELL. Well, that's completely ridiculous. Orla, why don't we head out for that walk?

>   (*But* **ORLA** *isn't listening, she's staring at* **CHERYL-ANN.** **NELL** *is panicking.*)

Really, this is just very upsetting now. Let's go. Orla?

>   (**ORLA** *is frozen to the spot but then slowly turns to* **NELL.**)

ORLA. What's going on?

NELL. What do you mean? Nothing. *Nothing.* This is total nonsense.

>   (**ORLA** *keeps looking at her.*)

ORLA. Nell... If there's something you need to tell me.

>   (*A horrible silence between the three of them.* **NELL** *is trying to decide what to do...*)

NELL. Orla...

ORLA. Oh God...

NELL. She arrived this morning.

ORLA. Okay.

NELL. She wanted to see me because...

ORLA. Because what?

NELL. She told me she had been with him.

ORLA. Who?

NELL. Robin.

ORLA. "With him" as in...

NELL. Yes.

ORLA. But how would they? How would she even know him?

> *(A pause.)*

NELL. She was his student.

ORLA. What? That can't be right. She never said... No. No, no, no. Sorry, no. Robin would never have done something like that.

NELL. That's what I said to her. I said that too.

ORLA. And I was just speaking to her, she mentioned a man called Jez...but not.

> *(The colour drains out of **ORLA**'s face.)*

Is that his baby? Is that why she came here?

NELL. She says that it is.

ORLA. I think I'm going to get sick. I'm going to get sick.

CHERYL-ANN. Can I get you a glass of water?

> *(They had both forgotten **CHERYL-ANN** was still in the room.)*

NELL. Do. And a bowl or something.

ORLA. No. Stop. Get her down here.

(A hesitation from **NELL** *and* **CHERYL-ANN**.*)*

NELL. Maybe you should get some fresh air first.

ORLA. *(To* **CHERYL-ANN**.*)* Bring her down here now.

CHERYL-ANN. Oh no, I don't want to get involved.

ORLA. Tough! You are now.

CHERYL-ANN. *(Quietly.)* Okay. I'll go get her.

*(***CHERYL-ANN*** slinks out of the room.* **ORLA** *is up now, pacing.)*

ORLA. Tell me everything you know.

NELL. I don't know much. She only arrived this morning. I had never seen her or heard of her before. She is clearly pregnant. She says she's seven months along. That's all I know. You were arriving, so I thought I'd...

ORLA. Hide her from me?

NELL. No!

ORLA. You were trying to keep her out of the house, you weren't going to tell me. That random tourist knew about it!

NELL. Orla, she had just arrived, I didn't have time to think. I wanted to make sure she was telling the truth.

ORLA. Why, do you think she's lying?

NELL. Well, we don't know her. This is the first time I've ever met her. But we do know him. Would he really do something like this?

ORLA. Just answer my question. Do you think she's making this up?

(A pause.)

NELL. No. I don't.

ORLA. Why's that?

NELL. She knew a lot about him.

ORLA. Like what?

NELL. Like how he was. And what mugs he used in his office. But she could know that anyway if he was just her teacher so... I don't know what to think.

> (**GABBY** *and* **CHERYL-ANN** *sheepishly enter the room.*)
>
> (*No one says anything for a moment.*)

ORLA. Is it true?

GABBY. I'm so sorry. I wish it never happened now. I really do.

ORLA. What did happen?

> (**GABBY** *pauses.*)

Tell me exactly.

GABBY. I was in his seminar group in September. And we just clicked. We just got on. And then we started talking a bit after class and I used to borrow books off him and then I'd go to his office to drop them back and then...

ORLA. And then what?

NELL. Orla, please. We don't need to go into the details.

ORLA. Oh, we do. Then what happened?

GABBY. Then one day we went for coffee and... I kissed him and then...that's when it started.

ORLA. How long did it go on for after that?

GABBY. Eh, a few months.

ORLA. What months exactly?

GABBY. I think the first time we got together was in October?

ORLA. My last miscarriage was in September. Great.

(**GABBY** *doesn't know what to say...*)

GABBY. He never mentioned anything about...

ORLA. And then you kept on seeing each other?

GABBY. Yeah, pretty regularly until maybe the end of term...

ORLA. So over Christmas?

GABBY. No. He had broken it off with me before Christmas, but we met up once again after that...

ORLA. Where did you meet up?

GABBY. In his office, mostly.

(**ORLA** *looks disgusted.*)

It wasn't a creepy thing, honestly. He didn't even want it to happen. I was the one who pushed it, honestly, I really did, and I knew it was wrong, I don't know what I was thinking now but I presumed you were...

ORLA. What?

GABBY. Someone different. Like, someone horrible, or something. Like I thought he was trapped in a marriage that was awful and sad.

ORLA. Did he tell you that?

GABBY. No. No. I guess I just thought that because it made sense to me at the time... But now I've met you and...you're not like that at all. I feel so unbelievably shit about it, I really do.

ORLA. Oh, that's great. Thank you for saying that you feel shit about it. That makes me feel so much better about having my ten-year marriage destroyed by a teenager.

GABBY. I'm twenty-one.

(*A beat.*)

Twenty-two in October.

*(A silence. **ORLA** turns to **NELL**.)*

ORLA. Is this really happening? After everything we've been through together. He lied to me. For months. How could he do that?

NELL. I don't know.

CHERYL-ANN. *(Piping up.)* Relationships are complicated, I guess.

*(**GABBY** puts her hand to her belly, she's feeling worse, she sits down, but no one notices this.)*

ORLA. You don't think I don't know that? I've been married for ten years. Together for fifteen. We had been through things together, we were, I *thought* we were a team. I mean, yes, things were difficult but...isn't everything that's worthwhile difficult at times?

(She asks this question to the room, but everyone is scared of opening their mouth now.)

But you stick it out, together. That's what's supposed to happen. It's not like we didn't have sex. I ovulated once a month, that's more than most married couples do it. I have it in a calendar. My God, his student...it's such a cliché. He's pathetic. He's disgusting.

NELL. Hang on now, Orla. He wasn't happy. Neither were you.

ORLA. So that's an excuse, is it? To sleep with his student?

NELL. I'm not saying that but maybe we can understand how –

ORLA. You never thought I was good enough for him.

NELL. What? Orla, it was the exact opposite; it was you who never felt *he* was good enough for you. You were always picking at him, trying to change him, never letting him be. If he had been enough for you, he probably wouldn't have had an affair.

ORLA. Of course this is my fault too. He's done everything right and I'm the one to blame, as usual.

NELL. You always expected so much from him. Not everyone has all these things that you think you should have by now.

ORLA. I know that. I am well aware of that.

NELL. Then how come from the moment you walked in that door you've been going on and on as if you're the only person who has ever lost someone? My only son died. He's gone. And all you can talk about is yourself.

ORLA. That's because he has ruined my life. If he was here right now, I swear to God I would make him feel...sooo bad. I would, I would...

> (*She is seething. Suddenly she picks up the box containing his ashes and starts to shake them.*)

Aaaah! You fucking prick! You bastard!!

NELL. Orla, No!

CHERYL-ANN. Oh my God!

> (**NELL** *grabs the ashes too and they wrestle over them.*)

NELL. Put him down!

> (**NELL** *desperately tries to tug the box away from* **ORLA**, *but it shockingly bursts open. Robin's ashes explode mostly onto* **NELL**. *A horrible silence. Everyone is stunned.*)

ORLA. I didn't... I didn't mean to –

> (**NELL** *is shaking with shock and despair.*)

NELL. This weekend was supposed to be about my son. And all the lot of you have done is make it about yourselves. I want you all out now. I don't want any of you under this roof where I raised him.

> (*She really means it, she's staring at them all, waiting for them to move.*)

ORLA. But where are we supposed to go?

NELL. I don't care! Get out. Now. Go on. Move!

CHERYL-ANN. Even me?

NELL. Especially you.

CHERYL-ANN. But where should we go?

NELL. I said I don't care. Sleep under a bush on the side of the road for all I care, I want you all out. Now.

CHERYL-ANN. I don't have anywhere else to stay.

ORLA. It's lashing rain.

CHERYL-ANN. We're in the middle of nowhere.

NELL. JUST GET OUT! I want to be alone with my son.

> (*Suddenly* **GABBY** *lets out a low moan. They all stop and look at her.*)

CHERYL-ANN. That doesn't sound good.

ORLA. What's wrong? What's happening?

GABBY. I don't feel very well.

ORLA. In what way?

GABBY. Painful.

ORLA. Painful, how painful? Where?

GABBY. In my belly. (**GABBY** *moans again.*) Uuuurgh.

(*A moment. Then* **ORLA** *kicks into action.*)

ORLA. Okay, this isn't good. Gabby, on a scale of one to ten how painful is it?

GABBY. TEN.

ORLA. We need to take her to hospital.

CHERYL-ANN. Should I call an ambulance?

ORLA. They'll take too long to get here. I'll drive her. Nell, I'll take your car.

CHERYL-ANN. Honey, can you stand up? We're going to get you to the car, okay?

GABBY. I'm going to wet myself.

ORLA. Don't worry about that. We'll put a towel down. Cheryl-Ann can you find something?

CHERYL-ANN. Sure can.

>(**CHERYL-ANN** *goes to the kitchen and finds a few tea towels.* **ORLA** *is helping* **GABBY** *up.* **GABBY** *is in pain and distressed, she's panicking now.*)

GABBY. I don't want to do this. I don't want to do this on my own.

ORLA. You won't be on your own. I'll be with you the whole time, okay? Gabby, look at me.

>(**GABBY** *manages to look at her.*)

Nothing bad is going to happen to you.

(*A moment between them.*)

Cheryl-Ann can you get her to the car? I'll get the keys.

CHERYL-ANN. Sure thing, here we go girl.

(**CHERYL-ANN** *helps* **GABBY** *out the door.*
ORLA *is looking for the keys, she finds them,
goes to leave then stops at the door and turns
to* **NELL**.)

ORLA. "Hospitable" is the word you were looking for
earlier. They told me my womb wasn't hospitable.

(**ORLA** *exits. Leaving.* **NELL** *alone, covered in
her son's ashes.*)

End of Part Two

PART THREE

(It's around four a.m. the following morning. There's a storm outside, wind and rain tapping at the windows. But over the following scene it clears as dawn breaks.)

*(**NELL** and **CHERYL-ANN** are sitting in the living room with a bottle of whiskey between them. They've been drinking. **NELL** has changed her clothes. They are silently staring into space. **CHERYL-ANN** is singing a slow, melancholic song. She's enjoying hearing her own singing voice...until **NELL** cuts her off.)*

NELL. Okay that's enough, thank you, Cheryl-Ann. Just need some quiet now.

CHERYL-ANN. Whatever you need.

NELL. *(Feeling bad.)* You do have a very nice voice though.

CHERYL-ANN. That's kind of you to say.

*(Back to silence again. **NELL** checks her phone.)*

Still nothing?

NELL. I think her phone is off. It's been going straight to voicemail. That, or she's blocked me.

CHERYL-ANN. I don't think she'd do that.

NELL. Really? After everything I said to her?

CHERYL-ANN. What about Gabby?

NELL. I don't even have her number. Do you?

CHERYL-ANN. I have her on Instagram. I'll check it.

NELL. I doubt she'd be posting about this. Unless she's one of those blogger people. Christ... I know nothing about her.

CHERYL-ANN. Her last post was a few months ago... Are you on Instagram?

NELL. Would you believe, I am.

CHERYL-ANN. What's your username? I'll follow you.

NELL. Nellandshep. N-E-L-L-A-N-D-S-H

CHERYL-ANN. Got ya. Three posts.

NELL. I'm not a very active member.

CHERYL-ANN. *(Holding up a picture she's examining.)* Is that him?

NELL. Yes. That's Robin.

CHERYL-ANN. Wow. Such a gorgeous smile.

NELL. That smile got him out of lots of trouble. Or in to, I should say.

CHERYL-ANN. Why did you call him Robin?

NELL. When I was pregnant with him, I kept noticing them around me all the time. It was like, this sounds ridiculous, but it was like they were keeping me company.

CHERYL-ANN. I totally get that. My sister sends me signs all the time.

NELL. Well, I don't mean they were signs just... I saw them a lot.

CHERYL-ANN. So get this, her full name was Jessica *Rose*. And after she died, I kept seeing single roses everywhere I went. On bushes, in windows, everywhere; lone roses. So, every time I see one, I think; there she is, saying hello.

(A beat.)

You think I'm crazy?

NELL. Well, it's a rose. What do you want me to say?

CHERYL-ANN. Sure, but they pop up everywhere. Even in the middle of winter. That's not normal.

NELL. Yes, but you're looking for them.

CHERYL-ANN. Yeah?

NELL. Well, that's problematic.

CHERYL-ANN. How so?

NELL. Because if you're looking for a sign, you're going to see a sign.

CHERYL-ANN. Exactly.

NELL. So you're just choosing to see things in a hopeful way.

CHERYL-ANN. I see nothing wrong with that.

(A pause.)

You're taking stuff right, medication?

NELL. Eh... No, I'm not.

CHERYL-ANN. You should try them. I know what you're thinking; Americans and medication, but I'm not one of those. After I lost my sister, they gave me a real leg up. And I was on the floor. As in, literally, I found myself lying face down on the kitchen floor at lot. Don't ask how I got there it just kept happening. Then one day, I think I had been there a few hours, and I swear to God, I heard her voice, crystal clear, saying "Cheryl-Ann, what the hell are you going to do now?" My first thought was how ridiculous I looked lying on the floor like that. And my second thought was she's right – what am I going to do now? Because this can't be it. So, I had to think about what I was really interested in, just me, which was hard because all my life, she called the shots. So, screw her, I applied for my passport and left the States for the first time, and you know what, it was so liberating. Even though it was hard as hell. It felt so good to do something just for me.

NELL. What happened to your sister?

CHERYL-ANN. Breast Cancer. She got it in her thirties and recovered. Then when it came back again, she went downhill pretty fast. It was about nine months.

NELL. Oh God...

CHERYL-ANN. Yeah. It was a cruel way to go. She was only forty-nine.

NELL. I'm so sorry. I know that's such a useless thing to say but I really am sorry for your loss.

CHERYL-ANN. I don't think it's useless. People mean it when they say it.

NELL. Sometimes... Were you close?

CHERYL-ANN. Oh, the closest. We lived together our whole lives since neither of us were very lucky in love. Sometimes when we went on vacation, we'd pretend we had husbands, we'd be like; "My God, it's good to get away from Rick and Nigel!" that kind of thing. We usually took a trip once a year, always in the States since Jess didn't like leaving the country. Yeah, we did everything together. I even went to all her chemo sessions with her, held her hand until the very end. And you know that part of our life, it wasn't too bad. I thought it was horrific at the time but now, compared to not having her here, it was kind of amazing. We laughed a lot during that time. She had a sense of humour that was dark as hell, I mean, seriously her jokes were not for public consumption.

NELL. Go on, tell me one.

CHERYL-ANN. There was this poor man called Jeff on the same ward, and he was so nice, really a very sweet guy, but he had this colostomy bag and Jess used to...no, really, she was a terrible person...but man, she knew how to make me laugh. Then when she couldn't speak anymore, we used to listen to the Harry Potter audio books together. Have you ever listened to them?

NELL. I haven't, no.

CHERYL-ANN. Side note; you should, they're amazing. I was in London before this and went to Kings Cross. Saw platform nine and three quarters. You ever been?

NELL. No. Kings Cross, yes, but not...the platform.

CHERYL-ANN. I was looking at all the crazies who were waiting in line to get their photo taken. And I thought, I want to do that too. So, I joined the line, and I asked this nice lady to take my picture and then I took one of her. And I'm so happy I did that. But I wished so much that she was there with me. Boy, do I miss her. She got me. You know what I mean?

NELL. I do. Robin and I, we got each other.

CHERYL-ANN. I had a feeling you did.

NELL. Or, at least, I thought we did... Did your sister ever let you down?

CHERYL-ANN. She didn't have an affair with a student if that's what you mean... But sure, Jess let me down all the time. In many ways she was a total nightmare. But still, not having that person anymore, the one who really gets you, it's lonely as hell.

NELL. I really am so sorry.

CHERYL-ANN. See? You mean it, I can tell.

> (*Suddenly they hear a noise coming from the hall.*)

NELL. They're back.

>(**ORLA** *enters on her own.*)

ORLA. Hi.

NELL. Hi...

ORLA. She's okay. Kidney infection.

NELL. And the baby?

ORLA. She's fine.

>(**NELL**'s *hand goes to her heart.*)

NELL. Oh, thank God. Thank God for that.

CHERYL-ANN. What a relief.

ORLA. You both stayed up?

CHERYL-ANN. We were worried sick.

NELL. We wanted to be up if you came back. I couldn't get through to your phone, so I didn't know what to do.

ORLA. Ran out of battery. Sorry.

NELL. So, what did they say?

ORLA. Very common apparently if you're not looking after yourself properly. Which she is most certainly not. I honestly think she's in complete denial about the whole thing.

NELL. Did she say anything about what she might do now?

ORLA. We didn't talk much. She was in a lot of pain, and she was terrified, so I didn't want to push it... Then she slept all the way back in the car.

NELL. She's here?

ORLA. Yeah, they discharged her. Once they gave her the IV antibiotics she felt better almost straight away. She just needs to rest now and keep taking her tablets.

NELL. That's a good sign if they sent her home?

ORLA.   Really good. They didn't seem worried. She's upstairs now, calling her mum.

NELL. Oh God, what'll her mum think.

ORLA. I have no idea...

NELL. What was she thinking coming over here on her own?

ORLA. I really don't know... You changed your clothes?

NELL. Yes, I did.

ORLA. I didn't mean to...

NELL. No, I know. I know. I'm just so glad she's okay.

ORLA. Yeah, me too.

NELL. And you?

ORLA. I'm fine.

CHERYL-ANN. You look like you could use a drink.

NELL. Yes, sit down.

> (**CHERYL-ANN** *pours her a drink.* **ORLA** *sits down.)*

ORLA. I'm not supposed to be drinking.

CHERYL-ANN. Why's that?

ORLA. But I have been.

> (*She takes a big gulp from a glass, winces at how strong it is, swallows it.)*

I hate driving in the dark.

NELL. You're very good to look after her like that.

ORLA. Well, someone had to, she's completely alone.

NELL. Still, given everything she's done...

ORLA. She was so scared in the hospital. And I realised I was holding her hand and it was like there was nothing between us, like she was just a girl who was alone and terrified, and I was the only person who could help her. I truly felt so sorry for her.

(*A beat.*)

What was he thinking?

NELL. I wish I knew.

ORLA. How can that be the same person I was married to?

NELL. I've been trying to get my head around it all night.

ORLA. I realised that when I was asking what you thought of my IVF plan you already knew about Gabby and the baby.

NELL. I had just found out.

ORLA. I feel so stupid.

NELL. Please don't.

ORLA. There I was desperately asking your permission to hope for something that you knew Gabby already had. Without even trying. Without even wanting it.

NELL. It's very unfair, I know.

ORLA. How many times do you think your heart can break?

NELL. I... I don't know.

ORLA. I saw her. The baby. On the Ultrasound. New life, you know, it always amazes me. How incredible it is. And then it made me think of trees. My four trees...

(*A silence.*)

Do you think he knew he was going to die?

NELL. What? Orla, no. Of course not.

ORLA. No. Just sometimes I feel as if we're all on these paths...you know...like our lives are set out in front of us and from the moment we're born everything has already happened. Like it was our destiny to be here. Like nothing I do can change anything that's going to happen. So, all this trying...it's so tiring. And for what? Because right now it all seems too risky.

NELL. What is?

ORLA. Loving someone. Having someone in your life who you can't bear to lose.

> *(They noise from the hall and* **GABBY** *sheepishly enters the room. They all shift a little.)*

GABBY. Hey.

NELL. Hey. Come on in. We're all so relieved you're okay.

GABBY. You didn't have to stay up or anything.

NELL. Of course we did.

CHERYL-ANN. We were so worried about you.

NELL. How are you feeling now?

GABBY. A lot better. Sorry about the fuss, bit embarrassing.

NELL. Nothing to be sorry for.

GABBY. Turns out it's just a kidney infection.

NELL. Orla said.

GABBY. Yeah, Orla was amazing. I don't know what I would have done if she wasn't there. Hospitals freak the shit out of me.

CHERYL-ANN. I get that.

ORLA. Did you speak to your mum?

GABBY. She didn't answer...probably not up yet.

CHERYL-ANN. I'd offer you a whiskey but...

GABBY. I'm pregnant, yeah. I know. I'm having a baby, turns out.

NELL. You are.

GABBY. They said it looks like it will be around the end of August. So I'll still get to go back to uni in September.

NELL. Right...that's good. Have you thought any more about what you want to do?

GABBY. Not really. Definitely want a lot of pain killers during the birth because that was fucking painful, and it wasn't even the real thing.

NELL. You can of course stay here as long as you like. We could sign you up to my GP and maybe get you seen by a local midwife.

GABBY. Yeah maybe...it's just very far away from everything. And after tonight, I don't know how I'd get to the hospital if I was on my own... Thank you, though. Sorry. This is such a mess, I know. I'm so sorry for coming here.

NELL. You have nothing to be sorry for. I'm glad you came.

GABBY. I thought if I came here, I would know what to do. Or I'd feel close to him again or like, I thought maybe he'd help me, in some way. And yeah, I wanted to see where he grew up. I wanted to see a little part of him. Guess I missed him a bit.

NELL. You missed him?

GABBY. It was so surreal, you know. That one minute he was here and then...not. He sent me a voice note the same day he died and I just kept listening to it over and over again to hear his voice. Because I never really felt like he was dead just...gone. I had other messages, but I deleted our history when he broke it off because I was so angry at him. I never thought that that would be the last thing I'd hear from him.

ORLA. What did it say?

GABBY. The voice note? Um, nothing really, just that if I was around, I could call in to his office. But when I did, he wasn't there. I thought he had just chickened out.

ORLA. I want to hear it.

GABBY. What?

ORLA. I want to hear the message.

GABBY. Eh. There's nothing really on it just –

NELL. Play it.

> (**GABBY** *looks at* **ORLA***, she doesn't say anything against it.*)

GABBY. Alright...

> (*They all wait, expectantly.* **GABBY** *finds it.*)

> (**ROBIN***'s voice plays out loud from her phone, he's on a noisy street:*)

ROBIN'S VOICE. "Hi Gabs...hope you're good. Just walked past a Subway and was thinking of you... Finally finished that book you leant me. If you wanted to pick it up, I'll be in the office until around seven? So, yeah, maybe see you later, if you're up for it, that is, no pressure... (*A long pause.*) Okay".

> (*A horrible, horrible pause.*)

NELL. Give me that.

> (*Meaning the phone.* **GABBY** *does so.* **NELL** *plays it again. Staring at the phone.*)

ROBIN'S VOICE. "Hi Gabs...hope you're good. Just walked past a Subway and was thinking of you... Finally finished that book you leant me. If you wanted to pick it up, I'll be in the office until around seven? So, yeah, maybe see you later, if you're up for it, that is, no pressure... *(A long pause.)* Okay".

(It stops playing. A silence.)

NELL. Was he nice to you?

GABBY. Of course, he was. You know what he was like, of course he was nice to me.

NELL. No, it's not 'of course'. It's not of course anything.

GABBY. Really, he wasn't –

NELL. He was your teacher. He was supposed to look after you. You could still be in the hospital right now. Something much worse could have happened to you.

GABBY. But it didn't. I'm fine.

NELL. He has let me down. Let Orla down, unimaginably. But Gabby, he's let you down the most. I am ashamed of what he's done.

GABBY. I'm not ashamed.

NELL. Then why haven't you told anyone about it?

(A pause. She's right.)

GABBY. I've told you.

NELL. A complete stranger. You said to me you didn't want your friends to think you were 'one of those girls' who gets pregnant.

GABBY. Yeah. I didn't mean anything bad just...you know what I mean.

NELL. I do know. I was around your age when I found out I was pregnant with Robin. And obviously it was a surprise, or an accident, however you want to put it. Which was problematic, to say the least. As well as the fact that I had nothing to do with the father. He was a complete stranger... He was just hitch-hiking around the West, and pitched his tent in a field across from the pub I used to pull the odd shift in whenever I came home. I was studying up in Galway at the time. We got chatting at the bar and spent the night together in his tent. And then we said goodbye the next morning after he made me breakfast – a tin of beans he heated up over a campfire. Then I snuck back home so early my parents didn't even know I was out. And it wasn't until weeks later I found out I was pregnant. He was long gone by then. We didn't have phones, well, landlines but not mobiles... I didn't even know his surname. Not to mind his address. He was Austrian. I had never met anyone from Europe before, imagine.

CHERYL-ANN. Was he handsome?

NELL. Very.

CHERYL-ANN. You must have been a real free spirit back then.

NELL. The sad thing is, I wasn't. Up until then I had done everything by the book. It was one night of recklessness and then came Robin. Feels like I'm telling you about a different person now. So long ago. Being pregnant back then was the worst possible thing that could happen to you. When I started showing people around here treated me like I had a disease. I remember leaving the shop one day and hearing a friend of my mother's, Nora Spillane, say "and she was such a good girl". I'll never forget that. She *was* such a good girl.

GABBY. What about your parents? Did they help you?

NELL. They did. They supported me. And of course, when Robin was born they adored him. But I broke their hearts when I told them. My father didn't look me in the eye until Robin was about six months old, barely said two words to me.

GABBY. Why not?

NELL. Because he was ashamed. I didn't blame him, you know. It was the eighties, they were very religious, and up until then I was their 'Golden Girl'. The funny thing was all that time he was avoiding me, he was also building an extension for me and Robin to live in. That's the barn now.

CHERYL-ANN. That sounds incredibly lonely. All of it.

NELL. It was. It really was. I have been sitting here tonight thinking what was all that shame for? Now, here we are, and the same thing has happened again and what's worse is that it's by my own son...the man who I raised. The person I love the most in the world...

> *(A pause.)*

So, whatever you do, do not be ashamed of this. Do you hear me?

> *(**GABBY** nods.)*

GABBY. I hear you.

NELL. You need to decide what to do for yourself and whatever you decide, it'll be the right thing to do.

> *(A phone starts buzzing.)*

GABBY. Oh my God. My mum is calling me back.

NELL. You should answer that.

> *(**GABBY** answers the phone and stands up to leave the room. We hear the first few lines she says to her mum on the phone:)*

Hi Mum! Yeah, I'm okay... Eh... I'm in Ireland... A place called Liscannor... No, no, I'm not alone.

> *(She leaves the room.)*

ORLA. I might head to bed. Been a long night.

NELL. Absolutely. You must be wrecked.

    (**ORLA** *gets up to go.*)

ORLA. About tomorrow…?

NELL. Yes. Tomorrow. I'd like to scatter him at the cliffs. There's a spot we used have picnics on when he was a boy. He loved watching the puffins jumping off the rocks.

ORLA. That's a lovely idea.

NELL. I was going to say a few words too if you didn't mind.

ORLA. Of course, I wouldn't.

NELL. I found this book I used to read him. It's about a little boy and his dog, called "I'll always love you". Maybe a bit silly, but it was either that or something from *The Modern Environmentalist*… Do you want to say something?

ORLA. I don't think there's anything to say.

    (*A pause.*)

I loved him, Nell. I really loved him.

NELL. I know you did.

ORLA. But our relationship was so worn down by sadness. And then he died. So now I'll never know what would have happened. All our plans, all our dreams, gone. And now this on top of everything… And, annoyingly, I still miss him. Even after all this.

NELL. You know, if this is too hard for you, you really don't have to come tomorrow.

ORLA. But you'll be on your own?

NELL. I'd understand.

    (*A pause.*)

ORLA. I'll think about it. Right now, I just need to sleep.

(**ORLA** *goes to the door.*)

NELL. Orla. No matter what, you're always going to be welcome in this house.

(**ORLA** *takes this in and then leaves the room.*)

CHERYL-ANN. You think she's going to be okay?

NELL. I don't know... But she's one of the toughest people I've ever met. So, there's that.

CHERYL-ANN. What about you? How are you doing?

(*A pause.*)

NELL. Do you ever get the feeling you've done your life completely wrong?

CHERYL-ANN. All the time. Look at me. What the heck am I doing here? I'm an adult woman who loves birds and Harry Potter. People think I'm nuts. I don't give a hoot. Because isn't that enough? To enjoy my time here and try not to hurt anybody. That's all I'm trying to do now.

(*A pause.*)

NELL. Would you like to stay on another few days? Free of charge, of course.

CHERYL-ANN. Are you kidding? Of course, I would.

NELL. I'm glad.

CHERYL-ANN. There's still a lot of birds I've yet to spot in this area. You wanna hear my list?

NELL. We should probably get some rest too.

CHERYL-ANN. Good idea.

(*They start to get up and reorder the room from the night's events.*)

(NELL brings their glasses over to the sink and catches the light shifting out of the window.)

NELL. It's almost morning.

CHERYL-ANN. Sunrise. Best time of the day to spot.

NELL. Can I ask you something?

CHERYL-ANN. Sure. Anything.

NELL. When does it start to feel better?

(Over this passage and the following lines until the end, the light gets brighter and brighter as NELL and CHERYL-ANN casually move towards the front of the stage. Sounds of herring gulls and weather can fade in and they are on the cliffs by the time CHERYL-ANN says "My God, it's beautiful".)

CHERYL-ANN. I wish I could tell you it does...but I'm a terrible liar. This feeling, this grief. It doesn't have an end. It doesn't resolve like in stories... But you're going to get bigger around it. And someday you'll feel like doing things again. Things that you might even enjoy. Sounds crazy. But it happens. And it might take a while but eventually something small will happen and you'll notice yourself feeling semi-okay again. And it could be anything, something random, like hearing your old favourite song on the radio or someone unexpected waving at you from their car. And you'll feel like, man, I'm really glad I stuck around.

NELL. I can't imagine it right now.

CHERYL-ANN. You don't have to. You just have to keep going. My God, it's beautiful.

NELL. Isn't it? Breathtaking.

CHERYL-ANN. Razorbill!

NELL. What?

CHERYL-ANN. I just saw a razorbill. Man, this is a good time of day to spot.

NELL. There's sometimes puffins along the cliff if you can bear to look down far enough.

CHERYL-ANN. They're going to be extinct soon, you know.

NELL. Is that, right?

CHERYL-ANN. By soon, I mean a hundred years or so.

NELL. Better spot them now then.

CHERYL-ANN. Oh hey, what's that little guy doing here?

NELL. A robin.

CHERYL-ANN. Well, how about that?

NELL. He's come to say hello.

(Blackout.)

End of Play

ABOUT THE AUTHOR

Erica is a playwright originally from County Limerick. She has a BA in Drama and Theatre Studies from Trinity College Dublin and an MFA in Playwriting from The Lir Academy. She is a previous member of the Six in the Attic scheme with the Irish Theatre Institute, the Soho Theatre New Writers course and the Lyric Theatre New Playwrights Programme. Her first play, *The Cat's Mother*, toured to London, Edinburgh and the Dublin Fringe Festival in 2018 where it won the Fishamble Award for Best New Writing and was nominated for the Stewart Parker Award. In 2019 she was the Channel 4 writer-in-residence at The Lyric Theatre, Belfast where her play *All Mod Cons* premiered. She also receeived the Sonia Friedman Award for her new play *The Magnificent*.